# PANCAKES
## BY
## PATRICK CHALMERS

## Patrick R. Chalmers

Patrick Reginald Chalmers was born in 1872, in Ireland. He worked as a banker, however is best known as a writer, encompassing various topics such as field sports (all sorts of hunting with hounds), deerstalking and horse racing. Chalmers also wrote well received biographies of Kenneth Graham, the Scottish author most famous for *The Wind in the Willows*, and J. M. Barrie, another Scottish author and dramatist, best remembered today as the creator of *Peter Pan*. Chalmers' first book, dedicated to his own writing, was *Green Days and Blue Days* (1912), followed by *A Peck of Malt* (1915).

As well as his substantial fictional and non-fictional oeuvre, Chalmers contributed to *Punch, or the London Charivari*, a highly influential British weekly magazine of humour and satire, established in 1841 by Henry Mayhew and engraver Ebenezer Landells. He also wrote for *The Field*, the world's oldest country and field sports magazine, having been published continuously since 1853. Chalmers used his expertise in outdoor pursuits to win a commission to edit the hunting diaries of Edward VIII, when he was the Prince of Wales. The then Prince was an enthusiastic hunter, making the task a mammoth undertaking for an already over-employed writer.

Chalmers also wrote much poetry, focusing on day-to-day Irish life, as well as hunting, fishing, cats and dogs. He died in 1942, at the age of seventy. As an interesting aside, a line from Chalmers' poem, 'Roundabouts and Swings', has now (in reversed form) passed into common parlance - although the origin is often no longer remembered.

*'An' a lurcher wise as Solomon an' lean as fiddle-strings*
*Was joggin' in the dust along 'is roundabouts and swings.'*

## CONTENTS

| | | PAGE |
|---|---|---|
| I. | The Return | 5 |
| II. | The Little Young Lambs | 7 |
| III. | The Undefeated Dryad | 8 |
| IV. | Nausicaa Speaks | 9 |
| V. | Fancy Dress | 10 |
| VI. | Chiron | 13 |
| VII. | Pott or Pan | 15 |
| VIII. | The White Boy | 17 |
| IX. | Hyacinthus | 20 |
| X. | Helen | 21 |
| XI. | The Idle Shepherdess | 23 |
| XII. | The Sandals | 25 |
| XIII. | Pegasus | 27 |
| XIV. | A Fallen Star | 29 |
| XV. | The Faun | 31 |

## I: THE RETURN

THE winds on earth pipe bugle free,
They've wakened sweet Persephone ;
She's stretched her ivory arms, has she,
   Her sea-blue eyes she's blinked ;
And " Oh ! " she's said, and " Oh ! " she's said,
" 'Tis time that I was out o' bed,
The rooks are building overhead,
   I dreamt 'em most distinct."

She doesn't wake her serving-maids,
Neat-fingered Phœbes of the Shades ;
She's brushed her hair in shining braids
   Bright gleaming as king-cup ;
She's laid her chiton out to don,
She's warmed her bath with Phlegethon ;
She's found her sandals, slipped them on,
   And hooked her own self up.

And now a-down the palace stair,
O'er coal-black marble huge and bare,
Behold her run, so rosy rare,
   And white as mayflowers fall ;
Low laughing in a roguish dread,
Down echoing corridors she's fled,
And " Hey for holidays ahead ! "
   Says she, and o'er the hall.

And now she stands on tip-toe's tip,
The big door's upper bolt to slip ;
And now, a finger laid to lip,
   The lower back she's shot ;
She's turned the great key, clanking clean,
And out she steps, our little Queen,
Who wonders just how bold she's been,
   And rather hopes a lot.

Now in the nether morning mute
She stands half shy, half imp acute,
To take the grim guards' clashed salute
   With most becoming mien ;
Then, prettier than I can tell,
She trips across the asphodel ;
While early ghosts she meets say, " *Well,*
   Of all things, there's the Queen ! "

And here she's come to Styx's flow,
Where an old puntsman (whom you'll know)
Says, " Goin' over, Miss ? Why so,
　　Just do'ee step right in ! "
And adds, good-willed as boatmen are,
" So Missy found the door a-jar
Once more ? My service to your Ma :
　　You'm lookin' peart's a pin."

Then o'er that rayless flood they glide,
And out she hops the homeward side,
And, " Thank you, Charon dear ! " she's cried,
　　" You'm welcome, Miss ! " bawls he,
As off, like swallow, see her fly,
And, as those little feet flit by
The crocus flames, a thrush on high
　　Shouts, " Here's Persephone ! "

　　　　　*　*　*　*　*　*

Child goddess of the daisy-chain,
If thus I've brought you home again
By Fancy led in Folly's train,
　　With liberty undue,
Forgive these vanities of song,
Poor dreams that to the bard belong ;
For, dream he right or dream he wrong,
　　Who cares if come you do ?

## II: THE LITTLE YOUNG LAMBS

      In the fold
      On the wold
There were little young lambs,
  An' the wind blew so cold
They laid lee o' their dams,
  An' a shepherd old man
He leaned over the cotes,
  An' a lilt he began
With a flutter of notes,
The little young lambs all among;
Oh, he piped 'em a derry down derry, he did,
  Since they were so young.

      An' they stirred
      When they heard,
Did the little young lambs,
  Then they hopped, most absurd,
From a-lee of their dams,
  An' they jumped and they skipped
With tip-toppetty skips,
  As the little tune tripped
From the reed at the lips
Of the crinkled old man o' the wold,
As he piped 'em a merry down derry, he did,
  Since he was so old.

      For he blew
      That he knew
Why the seasons went round,
  An' why green the wheat grew
To his pipe's pretty sound;
  An' why rain follows sun,
An' how sun follows rain,
  An' how everything's done
To be started again,
Till the stars like ripe acorns shall fall;
An' he piped 'em his derry down derry, he did,
  Along of it all.

## III: THE UNDEFEATED DRYAD

T H E team came down the middle ride,
The yellow, mellow middle ride;
The horses hauled with lurch and slide
    A new-felled forest oak;
And play-time, May-time West winds grew
From out the mild October blue,
And red leaves ran and gold leaves flew
    Like little forest folk.

And then, where once the tree had stood,
In splendid, ended state had stood,
Pale as a moonbeam in the wood
    I saw a dryad fair,
So slight and white and derelict;
A wood-mouse round her slim feet flicked;
But swift an acorn up she picked
    And melted into air.

" The pretty pagan thing ! " cried I,
" The magic *tragic* thing ! " cried I,
" By all I've read she ought to die,
    Her guardian giant gone;
They've dashed her, crashed her home to ground,
But she, the darling, looks around
And all among the wreck, she's found
    Fresh hope to carry on.

" And thus," said I to me, " I'll do,
'Gainst gods and odds and all I'll do,
When next my castles tumble, too,
    In fragments on the floor—
The ruin view in equal mind,
If not content at least resigned,
And haply 'mid the *débris* find
    The germ of one dream more."

And to the captious who conceive,
To flouters, doubters who conceive
A bard subsists on make-believe
    And dryads never were—
*A golden, olden Autumn wood,*
*For one who walks it as he should,*
*Shows many a shy unlikelihood,*
    *Holds many a ferly fair.*

## IV: NAUSICAA SPEAKS

THE man from the sea had the mien of an eagle,
  A bold eye of blue had the man from the sea,
The man from the sea had a tongue to inveigle
  A king and his council, and *me*, my dears, *me* ;
And he stood 'mid our folk like a sword among rods,
And he walked like a stag on the hills of the gods.

The man from the sea could charm palace or tavern,
  The man from the sea had the forehead of brass,
A laugh like the sea-wind a-shout in a cavern,
  And love for a wine-skin and eke for a lass,
And guile of a serpent to plot and to plan,
But, to carry him through it, the might of a *man*.

The man from the sea he had feasted and fasted,
  The man from the sea had both suffered and sung,
The years were his slaves which his manhood outlasted,
  He ne'er could be old, he had never been young ;
And the gleam of his smile through his bristle of beard
Was a thing to be loved—or a thing to be feared.

The man from the sea was a teller of stories
  Of giants and pirates, of sailors made swine,
Of storm and enchantment, the trail and its glories,
  White nymphs and soft islands in seas dark as wine ;
And always I heard him, and always I knew,
Though he lied when he listed, that here he told true.

He stood at the council and spoke with my father,
  As leader to leader, bold tongued, unafraid
(The members a-marvel his statecraft to gather,
  His sooths upon strategy, triremes or trade) ;
Men liked him, though after he'd dined with the Guards
'Twas thought he was just a bit lucky at cards.

But oh, when the moonlight fell softly and solemn
  He'd coax me aside lest my ladies should hear,
And, in the warm dusk of the porphyry column,
  He'd murmur the honey we maidens hold dear,
And whisper, " I love you, my beauty, my sweet,
Won't you help me (*there's* why) with a ship of the fleet ? "

I listened at last ; and Ulysses, the teller
  Of stories, by morn was a cloud on the blue ;
And, quitting the Court (and its half-empty cellar),
  He took (or I thought so) my heart with him too ;
But certainly gone were the pick of my pearls
And the daintiest darling of all of my girls.

## V: FANCY DRESS

The shepherd said, "I was merry a bit
   (Along o' the Fair befall?),
Or I'd never a' tried or attempted it—
   Two hundred o' ewes an' all—
Or I'd never ha' wagered to drive a flock
With devil a dog to the Knowes o' Knock.

"But where was a readier lad, you'd hold,
   Than me at twenty-four?
My cheek was brown and my eye was bold,
   And I stood as high as the door;
I've picked a ewe under either arm
And carried 'em in from fold to farm;

"And every lass when the sheep came down,
   'Ud turn at Oliver Rigg,
In the wet grey streets o' the market town,
   So bonny an' clean-built big,
And tell 'emselves, 'Yon's the gradely chap,
From the sole o' his brogues to the crown o' his cap!'

"Well, 'twas Fair-time, same as I've said afore,
   And I took Ben Mogg's half-quid
That I'd drive two hundred o' ewes, an' more
   (And I tried, by all, I did),
With never a wave or wag of a dog—
But he won his money, did Benjamin Mogg.

"Eight miles to go to the Knowes o' Knock,
   But the moon was nigh at full,
And me as full as a fighting-cock
   And strong as a yearling bull;
Eight miles to walk 'em, the Roman's Way,
And deliver 'em sound by break o' day.

"I slipped the rails and I walked 'em through,
   As the summer dusk split o'er,
They were fell-land bred and they kind o' knew
   They were due for the fells once more;
And they powdered on in a pattering mob;
For the first two miles 'twas a baby's job.

"But when we'd gotten to Garcross Ring,
    And the unfenced grass again,
They broke like beads from a broken string,
    While I sweated and swore like Cain;
For some broke this way and some broke that,
Some took the fell side and some the flat.

"Thinks I, we'll never make out to Knock,
    When white as a moonbeam came
A fine tall maid in a moon-white frock;
    She moved like a wind-blown flame
In her queer strapped shoes; she was bare o' head;
'A visitor up at the Grange,' I said.

"And a duchess, too, you'd imagine, Sir,
    And finely bred as few;
And she'd two long dogs at the side o' her,
    And she carried a long bow, too;
And a shimmery moon in her hair, no less—
Well, the gentry's crazy on fancy dress.

"'Will I lend you a hand?' she says to me,
    'For I've known a shepherd of old,
And I've turned the buck and the roe,' says she,
    'So sheep'll be light to fold;
'Yes, I knew a shepherd,' she kind of sung;
'He looked like a god when the gods were young.'

"She spoke a word and her greyhounds sped
    With a wrench and a racing sweep,
And they packed the ewes where the grass-track led
    As though they were bred to sheep;
Then, a bit too fast, though, to take a flock,
They worked 'em over the dale to Knock.

"And she talked the while, so kind, so grand,
    And her voice was like woods in Spring,
And she told of a hill in a mountain land
    Till her eyes were the stars that sing;
So deep were her eyes, with their fire and ken,
That I've never looked much at a lass since then.

"She bade me go at the carse o' Knock;
    But I says, 'Your grace,' says I,
'You've helped a shepherd lad drive a flock

Through half of a night—now why?'
She spoke a riddle, she laughed, 'O dunce,
For the love o' your brother on Lat Moss once!'

\*      \*      \*      \*      \*

"I paid Ben's money come market day,
   And he stood me a quart—Ben Mogg;
I said I'd had a hand on the way
   From a mate with a likely dog;
But I never said how 'twas a queen, to Ben,
And I've never spoke much with a lass since then."

## VI: CHIRON
### *An Idyll*

CHIRON the wise, the kindly,
  He tutored the sons of kings;
And Youth it followed him blindly
  And learnt of the seemly things,
    The sword and the song that rings;
Of strife and sport and the glory
  Of life, so the wise words fell;
But Chiron's only a story;
  Well, here is a tale to tell.

Or ever their days grew weighty,
  There walked companions four;
The sum of their years was eighty
  And each had achieved a score—
    Would any man ask for more?
They'd fire for the Thames—a-plenty,
  They'd planets to set a-spin;
We were all of us kings at twenty
  When kingdoms were still to win.

The road from the coast they'd taken,
  The sea and the day behind;
They'd stopped and they'd sliced the bacon
  A-top of the downs and dined,
    On cushiony thyme reclined;
Five miles from the pier and pierrots;
  And the lights of the front stood bright
Ere they picked up their packs like heroes
  To walk through a short June night.

The scut of a bolting bunny,
  The green of a glow-worm's spark,
Made play, till a moon like honey
  Rolled up on a down-ridge stark,
    And conquered the violet dark;
And the way was afire with wonder
  Where the ivory may-trees ran
To a shadowy shaw, and under
  Its lee stood a caravan.

The wheels were a sun-cracked yellow,
  The body was gipsy gay,
And by sat a mighty fellow

Who pulled at a purring clay
    That reeked to the Milky Way;
But he spoke like a host and scholar
    As he rose in polite ado,
While his old horse, free of the collar,
    Strolled up to be civil, too.

He tossed them a Greek quotation,
    He dropped into Homer sheer;
But he poured them a tramp's libation
    Of marvellous bottled beer
    That winked to the moonshine clear;
And he spoke of the stars in Heaven,
    And the Marquess of Queensberry's Rules,
And he told of a stag in Devon
    And of trout in a hundred pools.

And he leaned on the horse's shoulder,
    And the great horse, stamping, stood,
While he spoke of the spark a-smoulder,
    The flame in the kindled wood,
    Of rhyme and of hardihood;
And the four of them heard him, gazing;
    And to one, ere the words were done,
In the dim and the mad moon's mazing,
    The horse and the man seemed one.

And the downs in the dark were humming
    Like sweeping of silver strings,
But here was the slow dawn coming
    With homely happenings,
    And songs that the stonechat sings;
And " None o' you *talk* for toffee,"
    Quoth he of the caravan;
" Hi, sticks for the fire, boys, coffee !
    'Tis time that to-day began."

Chiron the wise, the kindly,
    He tutored the sons of kings,
And Youth it took to him blindly
    And learnt of the splendid things,
    The bow and the harp that rings.
But now was the East a glory,
    The Channel a welt of gold;
Well, Chiron's naught but a story,
    And here is a story told.

## VII: POTT OR PAN

LAST June I walked to Wantage Town
By wold and oak-woods green of gown,
All emptily the blue bent down
    Save for the soaring haggard;
Then, just beyond the Roman Camp,
I met, half gipsy and half tramp
(I own a weakness for his stamp),
    A most amusing blackguard.

A tan-faced rascal, prone to ale
And, one might guess, nor greatly fail,
Acquainted with the County Gaol,
    Fifty and not too cleanly,
Yet with an eye, as you'd aver,
For maids—or hares as might occur;
He touched his cap and called me " Sir,"
    And said he'd tramped from Henley.

But did I wish to see a sight?
I countered with " Perhaps I might."
He led through hawthorns scattered white;
    " And now," quoth he, " keep quiet ";
And in a hollow, at their ease,
Enfolded in the downs' grey seas,
I saw as playful as you please,
    Five little fox-cubs riot.

They struggled in a knot of fur,
Then broke, like beads of quicksilver,
Paused, listened, and without demur
    Incontinently tumbled
Into their earth and jostled down—
Five little fox-cubs fat and brown;
" Worth sixpence each? Say half-a-crown ? "
    He said. I bowed and fumbled.

He spat on it for luck; said he,
" I likes all such young things to see;
I owns all Earth (but takes 2d.
    For buying beer and so on);
Sheepfolds I loves an' full barn floors,
A sun that warms, a wind that roars,
An' kissing wenches at back-doors."
    " No way," said I, " to go on.

"You're fifty (that's as sure as fate),
You badger-pied old reprobate;
But what's your name, at any rate,
   And how d'you get your living?"
He said, "I tramps from shire to shire,
And sometimes takes a harvest-hire;
But mostlywise—well, you'd admire
   How fond folk be o' giving.

"An' named? Well last time that the beak—
(Injustice, Sir, ain't far to seek;
I'd *found* the pheasants, so to speak,
   I'd got a rightful answer)
The Sergeant bawls out, 'Sylvan Pott,'
An' 'e should *know* now, should 'e not?
But times ago—I've half forgot—
   I've heard the name was Pan, Sir."

"O-ho!" cried I, "then hail and thanks,
Old hero of a hundred pranks,
Old antic with the hairy shanks,
   Who loved and larked and liquored;
Pipe us of Syrinx. How looked she,
That rosy rogue, your Omphale?
And Hercules—but pardon me—"
   Self-consciously he'd snickered.

He leered and touched his greasy cap
And turned to seek some ale-house tap,
A merry blackguard of a chap
   Howe'er you'd have him christened,
That whistled as he went a tune
Old as the downs and sweet as June.
A sheep-bell *clonked* across the noon;
   A hare sat up and listened.

## VIII: THE WHITE BOY

I STOPPED beside the halted caravan
    To hear the gypsy-talk
O'er wayside kettle, where the long road ran
    On like a javelin ever o'er the chalk
To the far Southdowns and the sounding sea
    (And so, I've heard it said, to Babylon,
    Carthage, tall Troy, e'en haunted Helicon);
I listened to the yarns they spun for me,
    Nor marvelled that, horse-copers all, of course,
    Ever the tales kept twisting back to *horse*.

I heard of changeling foals and " borrowed " sires,
    And deals of gypsy dare,
From Minehead and New Forest to the Shires,
    North to the Dales and back, by Barnet Fair,
To Epsom Downs, the Mecca of the clan;
    Learnt of the *whisper;* of horse-doctors heard
    Who healed by virtue of the spoken word;
And ne'er the tellers blushed beneath their tan;
    Then on from horse to horseman, old and new,
    Chifney to Archer, Sloan to Donoghue.

And, speaking of some giant of the craft,
    His courage, power and skill,
" He'd take," I cried, " a youngster, dancing daft,
    And in a twinkling smooth him to his will
By voice and hands, and that that's in you bred
    That makes the horsemaster, gentle yet bold,
    Sitting like Centaur " (platitude of old !)
" Who's *Centor*, then ? " young Jethro Cooper said;
    And so I told of Chiron and the rest.
    " Brother," said Jasper Lee, " we'll give you best."

But Abram Cooper, taking pipe from gums,
    On ninety nomad years
Looked back, and in his old, old tones, " It comes,"
    He said—" it comes to me, my dears,
How I did hear black Ephraim Cooper say,
    Long years ago, and he a horsewise chap,
    That he had seen, or heard on now, mayhap,
Just suchlike antic somewheres Lyndhurst way
    With Forest ponies; 'twas at rounding-up,
    I've heard him tell, when coves 'ud sit to sup.

"But whether 'twas himself was there or not,
   Or if 'twas story told
Mayhap to him by some'un, I've forgot,
   For why, you see, I'm old, my dears, I'm old ;
But 'twas the Forest and, he'd say, July,
   The opens red with heather, gold with whin.
Fine place the Forest to be campin' in,
   And fine to smell warm bracken, saddle high,
   And round her artful ponies, mob by mob,
Gallop and shout and whip-crack—verderer's job.

"Well, so he'd say, with one gay-going troop
   A colt, or summat, ran,
And on it, seemed, a boy sat cock-a-whoop,
   Bare as the breeze and white as milk in pan ;
He led with artifice his scampering lot
   Through clearing, thicket and wise groves of oak ;
   'Men never get close up to 'em,' said folk ;
'But when we *does* my lord'll catch it hot ! '
Shooting with arrows, too, 'twas told, the limb !
The verderer said he'd card the hide off him.

"And still the days wore on, the round got done,
   And still that mob went free ;
They never caught fair up with it ; they'd run,
   With that queer leader flashing white to see
From middle up, through the great Forest trees
   And sunny spaces, bright as butterflies ;
   None o' the talent, *gorgios chals* or *ryes*,
Got near to 'em or put 'em out of ease ;
   You'd gallop the long rides, then, mad perplexed,
   You'd see those shoeless heels flip down the next.

"One noon, so Ephraim told (if so 'twas he)—
   One noon of smoking heat,
He lay in the sweet fern, a-doze, maybe,
   And, waking, heard the tap of light hooves' beat ;
Then, through the broken sunlight, down the glade
   Walked that gay lot, heads tossing, pacing light,
   With snort and whicker ; playful lift or bite
Among the young 'uns. Sons, he was *afraid*,
   For with 'em came the White Boy, and, my oath,
   'Twas neither boy nor colt ; and yet 'twas both !

" A sorrel colt, hoof, hide and tail ; King's word,
    A dandy specimen,
But from the shoulder, rising white as curd,
    The belt-up body of a brat o' ten,
Cool-eyed and impudent ; and all on wire
    As any pony. One hand swung his bow,
    The other twitched, young mischievous, just so,
        The long tail of a two-year-old entire.
A strange and oddly sight to see 'em pass,
*That* and the ponies, down the sun-splashed grass.

" Sudden the Thing sensed *man*, and round it flung,
    It and the mob, like *that* ;
And as they wheeled a little arrow sung
    Past Ephraim's ear into a sapling, *pat* ;
Then off they went, manes flying, tails a-cock,
    Bucking and squealing, raising Harry Cain,
    Through the big oaks, to There-and-Back-again,
Like squibs and crackers or young Forest stock ;
    And Ephraim watched 'em go—fair shook he stood—
    Into sun-dazzle and blue belts of wood.

" There's no clear end. I've heard the mob was got
    Come the next rounding tide ;
The Boy was seen a bit, and then was not,
    But never *close* like. Most said Ephraim lied,
Was drunk or dreaming ; so it might ha' been ;
    But, mugged or sober, middling sound was he,
    And Romany don't lie to Romany.
If flesh ran there, I reckon he'd ha' seen
    One of our Brother's breed o' man-and-horse ? "
Knocking my pipe out, I replied, " Of course."

## IX: HYACINTHUS
### *(In February)*

In Autumn's dearth
Of warmth and mirth,
Take of kind earth
   The fill of bowl,
And in it lay
Fair bulbs, and say,
" To this mere clay
   Be living soul."

And now, behold,
Ere green and gold
To wood and wold
   Abroad entice,
Pinks, whites and blues
Do fill your cruse
With scents and hues
   Of Paradise.

In close-knit twirls
Of waxen curls
Each head unfurls
   Beloved, apart;
Becurled, I'd add,
To match the lad
Of old who had
   Apollo's heart.

Can bard do less,
Then, than confess
The loveliness
   That doth belong
To flowers that stand
For Beauty, and
By his command,
   Our Lord of Song?

Could column rare
A grief more fair
Lift into air
   From graven plinth?
Could love be lit,
By flame more fit,
More exquisite,
   Than Hyacinth?

" A sorrel colt, hoof, hide and tail ; King's word,
    A dandy specimen,
But from the shoulder, rising white as curd,
    The belt-up body of a brat o' ten,
Cool-eyed and impudent ; and all on wire
      As any pony. One hand swung his bow,
    The other twitched, young mischievous, just so,
      The long tail of a two-year-old entire.
    A strange and oddly sight to see 'em pass,
    *That* and the ponies, down the sun-splashed grass.

" Sudden the Thing sensed *man*, and round it flung,
    It and the mob, like *that* ;
And as they wheeled a little arrow sung
    Past Ephraim's ear into a sapling, *pat* ;
Then off they went, manes flying, tails a-cock,
    Bucking and squealing, raising Harry Cain,
    Through the big oaks, to There-and-Back-again,
Like squibs and crackers or young Forest stock ;
    And Ephraim watched 'em go—fair shook he stood—
    Into sun-dazzle and blue belts of wood.

" There's no clear end. I've heard the mob was got
    Come the next rounding tide ;
The Boy was seen a bit, and then was not,
    But never *close* like. Most said Ephraim lied,
Was drunk or dreaming ; so it might ha' been ;
    But, mugged or sober, middling sound was he,
    And Romany don't lie to Romany.
If flesh ran there, I reckon he'd ha' seen
    One of our Brother's breed o' man-and-horse ? "
    Knocking my pipe out, I replied, " Of course."

## IX: HYACINTHUS
### (*In February*)

In Autumn's dearth
Of warmth and mirth,
Take of kind earth
   The fill of bowl,
And in it lay
Fair bulbs, and say,
" To this mere clay
   Be living soul."

And now, behold,
Ere green and gold
To wood and wold
   Abroad entice,
Pinks, whites and blues
Do fill your cruse
With scents and hues
   Of Paradise.

In close-knit twirls
Of waxen curls
Each head unfurls
   Beloved, apart;
Becurled, I'd add,
To match the lad
Of old who had
   Apollo's heart.

Can bard do less,
Then, than confess
The loveliness
   That doth belong
To flowers that stand
For Beauty, and
By his command,
   Our Lord of Song?

Could column rare
A grief more fair
Lift into air
   From graven plinth?
Could love be lit,
By flame more fit,
More exquisite,
   Than Hyacinth?

## X: HELEN

WHEN Helen went to Egypt, old Father Time was young;
When Helen went to Egypt and held hearts in thrall,
    She was Love without leaven,
      A song that is sung,
      A goddess fresh from Heaven
    To walk mankind among;
And Egypt was Egypt, proud Egypt an' all.

When Helen went to Egypt, then all who saw her said,
" She's sea-foam and roses, the Queen from the North;
    Amid our princesses
      She's white and rose-red,
    And sunshine are the tresses
      That coil her lovely head,
And her eyes are blue lotus on Nilus brought forth."

When Helen went to Egypt, proud Pharoah down bowed he,
" By Pasht and by Isis she's all things ! " he vowed;
    And feast and good drinking
      Lost flavour and glee,
    And he couldn't sleep for thinking
      Of the Queen from the sea,
And her eyes of blue lotus—tall Pharoah so proud.

When Helen went to Egypt came wizards big and bold
To cure by their magic proud Pharoah the king,
    Who turned from the bright wine,
      The sound wine and old,
    The red wine and the white wine
      In goblets all of gold,
Because a sweet lady was lovely as Spring.

They mixed him of dark magics with pestle and pot,
But magic out of Sparta was roses and snow;
    Strange serpents they made him—
      Bright coil and gold spot,
    But Helen's gold hair swayed him
      And round his heart they got,
The bright coils of Helen that fell sandal-low.

All tales should find endings, and the told tales do,
  But this tale is secret to Sphinx and to Fate.
      I sing a beginning ;
        If only I knew
     The rest I'd stay song-spinning
       All night, to sing for you
The Rhyme of Sweet Helen and Egypt the Great.

But when Helen went from Egypt (so the old wives deem),
  A workbox One sent her with day-dreams wound in skein,
     That, when she sat stitching
      And sewing a seam,
     She might, at old sakes' witching,
      Sew in thereof and dream
Of Egypt, proud Egypt, crowned Egypt again.

## XI: THE IDLE SHEPHERDESS

In Arcady a shepherdess, neglectful of her flocks,
Would dance beneath a cypress in the flimsiest of smocks;
Her eyes were blue as gentians, and she used them on the shepherds,
While half her lambs were carried off by lynxes and by leopards,
As she danced beneath the cypresses and idled with the shepherds.

And Pan's own self he piped for her on merry reeds a-row,
And she danced her bonny hair down and she danced her cheeks aglow,
And she danced her wreath all crooked—down came buttercup and daisy;
In fact, apart from playing, she was lazy, lazy, lazy;
But her little foot fell lightly as a buttercup or daisy.

But Juno of Olympus, a severe and jealous dame,
Saw her dancing, always dancing, like the flickering of a flame,
And she said, " The little baggage, she deserves to get a slapping,
For her hands are always idle and her feet forever tapping;
Had I time for mundane matters I should *see* she got a slapping."

As it was, she took a thunderbolt from Zeus's box of tricks,
And blew the pretty shepherdess across the gloomy Styx,
And bade her be with Pluto and work out her own salvation;
" And your hands shall do the tapping in your next reincarnation;
Your fingers, not your feet," said she, " shall be your soul's salvation."

Now, Time, he's swept his scythe round and he's twirled his glass about,
And my shepherdess is working of her own salvation out;
Her Arcady forgotten, and the shepherds, and the piping,
'Tis her fingers tap the hours by, for, in fact, she's doing typing;
And she's excellent at shorthand, she who once heard Pan a-piping!

Her hands are quick and capable; if still the gentians lurk
'Neath her lashes, scarce you'll see them, for they're always on her work;
And she's highly confidential and self-confident and zealous,
And she hears a hundred secrets she would die before she'd tell us;
For she's very confidential and discreet as she is zealous.

But always, come the Springtime (e'en in Eastcheap come it will),
There's a violet on her table or a yellow daffodil,
And, walking to the office, with the neatest of umbrellas,
Her foot still falls like blossom from the wreaths she wove in
    Hellas.
(Did you ever see a wood-nymph with the neatest of umbrellas ?)

But Time, he swings his sickle and he twirls his glass, does he,
And, her expiation over, Juno soon may set her free ;
Shall we wed her to a viscount with a mansion in the West End,
A director of her company ? Perhaps 'twould be the best end.
I expect she'd *like* a viscount, with a ball-room in the West End
And a cypressed lawn in Sussex. Yes, most likely that's the best
    end.

## XII: THE SANDALS
### (*A tale for Shrove Tuesday*)

FAIR was the nymph Corinda's face,
  Her eyes were bright as candles,
A coy, capricious, woodland grace
  Untaught in classic scandals;
Blue violets in her hair had she,
White kirtle fell to whiter knee,
And ne'er a nymph in Arcady
  Could wear such little sandals—

Little, but stoutly wove withal
  In golden straw and pretty;
Of proof where slim pine-needles fall
  Or brookside beach is gritty;
So see her trip, 'mid pines and rills,
Adown the blue Arcadian hills,
Her fingers full of daffodils
  And on her lips a ditty.

The goat-foot god, that antic old,
  Stealing through copse and cover,
He saw and loved her, for, behold,
  To see her *was* to love her;
And surely he had fair excuse
To blow his reeds with roguish ruse,
Sweet notes, sweet notes, too oft the noose
  That snares such artless plover.

But not, at once, our heroine;
  Close goat-foot comes and closer,
But, murmurous deep or elfin thin,
  Not yet his pipes engross her;
Deft doth the god, now fast, now slow,
Entreat her, silverly and low,
Through the dim woods—the nymph laughs, "No,
  Old Hoofs-and-Horns, oh, no, Sir!"

"Yet shall she yield!" in pique thereat
  Pan vows by him who handles
Love's armoury, the wingèd brat
  Whom Aphrodite dandles;
Corinda o'er her shoulder threw
The witchery of eyes of blue
And mocked, "Good Faunus, an' I do,
  By Zeus I'll eat my sandals!"

But forthwith, fox in prankish craft,
    Pan prays the Boy, the bender
Of bow that speeds the kindling shaft,
    His quiver's best to send her;
Young Mischief takes him joyous aim;
Down comes his lovely laughing game,
Who, dimpling all in rosy shame,
    (In short) makes sweet surrender.

Laid is the feast on dewy lawn,
    When lo, what jovial thunder
Sets satyr, oread and faun
    Agape in awe and wonder?
The echo rolls from hill to hill—
" An oath on Zeus e'en nymphs fulfil;
*Her sandals bride Corinda will*
    *Eat here and now thereunder.*"

They're doffed, they're dished (to those dictates
    Must bow the most capricious),
And served—but *sandals?* golden cates
    Adorn a plate auspicious!
So Pan hath changed them, nothing loth
To mock his lord; and thus her oath
Corinda kept, and ate them both
    And found them quite delicious.

While on Olympus kindly Zeus,
    Beneath his azure rafter,
Espied afar that forest ruse
    With shout of jolly laughter,
And straightway said it that a meat
That's light as fall of little feet
And slim and gold and trim and sweet
    Should be Pan's cakes thereafter.

So now, if pancakes crown the feast,
    Be no unclassic vandals;
Remember Father Pan at least
    And that rapt reed he handles;
Recall Corinda, say that she
Was rosiest nymph in Arcady,
And name, in compliment to me,
    This story of her sandals.

## XIII: PEGASUS

LIKE a star descending on
The calm heights of Helicon,
Free of bridle, free of girth,
Dropped the wingèd horse to earth;
      Came he thus
The sky-coursing Pegasus.

Down he swept in spirals through
Jove's immensity of blue;
Now his hoof hath struck the sward
And, like leap and flash of sword,
      Waters throng
Bubbling with the soul of Song.

Kings and rich men, I've heard say,
" Silver Pegasus," said they,
" We've got money without end,
Be our magic horse, O friend ! "
      But the steed
Flung his heels and didn't heed.

Walked a herd-boy (hear my tale),
Seeking, in a Dorian dale
Where the stone-pine breathed above,
For a fitting rhyme to " love ";
      Velvet, bland,
Dropped a muzzle in his hand.

Turning then he saw (of course,
As you've guessed) the wingèd horse,
Mounted him, and at a bound
Reached those heights where Rhyme is found;
      Ripple clear
Tripped the ditty of his dear.

As he got him down again
On the humdrum homely plain,
Pegasus addressed him thus;
Comradely spoke Pegasus,
      And the youth
Learned this old, this equine sooth :—

"Money makes the mare to go
Where you want her, fast or slow;
Money drives a million things,
Never, though, the horse with wings
On the azure road, where 'love'
Rhymes triumphantly with 'dove';
*He*, unlike the aforesaid mare,
Goes by fasting and by prayer."
      Thus and thus
Spoke the cloud-white Pegasus.

## XIV: A FALLEN STAR

'Twas scarcely Autumn yet awhile,
Yet, as I stepped the homeward mile,
The spindles' warm autumnal style
    In hedgerows kindled,
And leaf and berry manifold,
Scarlet and crimson, chrome and gold,
Caught colour from the crisping cold
    As daylight dwindled.

Home sailed the rooks with distant cries.
I saw a farmstead's smoke arise
(Like incense of a sacrifice)
    On skies of dapple,
And a tall woman on the hill
Wished me Good-night, as wanderers will,
A strapping, fine, well-favoured Jill
    Who munched an apple,

With teeth as white and zest as keen
As though her years were but fifteen,
Instead of—well, she might have been
    What age you fancy;
Yet she'd the movement, she'd the air;
Coarsened, o'er-blown, the rose was there,
And, challenging the crows'-feet, were
    Strange eyes of pansy.

" Good-night," she said, " young man," anew;
I paused politely, as was due;
You'll like to be " Young man " when you
    Are forty-seven.
Deep was her voice, like bells a-far
(" *Mummer* " thinks I, " you've been or are ");
" Shepherd," she kind of cooed, " a Star
    Has fallen from heaven—

" A Star that once from Cyprian seas
(That sparkling blue, that sunlit breeze!)
Reigned, girdled queen of shepherd's pleas,
    On hills o' Summer,
Who now upon the pike must pad
And age a bit, still likes a lad
To talk to, though he says she's mad,
    Some broke-down mummer.

" For how grew star, or goddess, old ?
Why, bless his innocence untold !
When Love took second place to gold
    Came a grey hair of it ;
I never was the one to be
The understudy, so, you see,
I took me to mortality
    In piqued despair of it,

" And learnt to like a coin myself,
Folk must ha' something on the shelf
When there themselves, and I'm no elf
    To share with finches
The dew-fall or this hedgerow clutch
Of blackberries—no, not by much ;
Mortal am I, and sip of such
    That suits my inches.

" But still I love the apples, though,
And where the full boughs bend a-glow
I stop and beg one as I go
    For an old story
Of how a golden pippin's grace
Of old, on Ida's lordly chase,
Gave Loveliness the pride o' place
    From Power and Glory."

And " Thanks," says I, " 'tis clear enough,
They've taught you more than common stuff,
To hold me listening to such duff
    While tea gets cooler ;
Now I'm for home, yet at your shrine
Permit this votive gift of mine,
King George's head, in silver fine,
    A fellow-ruler ? "

But, as I went a-down the hill
Where sleepy finches twittered still,
Some sacred fowls, her sparrows shrill,
    Raised sudden rally ;
Yet on the turquoise of the West,
Afar, in gentle silver dressed,
Winked Venus' self, crowned and at rest,
    As usually.

## XV: THE FAUN

THE Faun piped in the coppice,
  He piped a plaintive strain;
I called on him to stop his
  "*Sweet Summer, come again!*"
Said he, "I pine for posies,
  For June in wood and wold;
The nymphs have got red noses
  And all the world's a-cold!"

"Come, ring a ring of roses,"
  Quoth I, "my bonnie lad;
Though nymphs have got red noses
  There's balm in Gilead;
Though frosty breezes rack us
  Through forests all forlorn,
I know a nook where Bacchus
  Fills high the jolly horn.

"Come, though the rude North bellows,
  I know a rosy inn
Where certain sound good fellows
  Sip sunshine from the bin,
True knights of malt and vine, Faun,
  Who'll reck not of attire
In any friend of mine, Faun,
  About the tap-room fire."

He came, he drained the rummer
  Of friendship and accord;
He swore 'twas always summer
  When Bacchus is the lord;
And, ring a ring of roses,
  He didn't care a jot
If nymphs had got red noses
  Or whether they had not.